South Moor and District
in old picture postcards

by the South Moor Local History Group

European Library ZALTBOMMEL/THE NETHERLANDS

GB ISBN 90 288 6282 x

© 1996 European Library – Zaltbommel/The Netherlands

No part of this book may be reproduced in any form, by print, photoprint, microfilm or any other means, without written permission from the publisher.

Introduction

This book has been compiled by members of the South Moor Local History Group. It is a pictorial account of the growth of the district when coal mining was the major industry. We hope we have achieved this within the limitations of 76 photographs. South Moor is part of the town of Stanley in North Durham, situated 9 miles north-west of Durham City and 11 miles south of Newcastle. Local directories state the area of South Moor, Craghead and Burnhope were in the Parish of Lanchester until 1865, when they came under the Parish of Holmside. This was the ancient seat of the Tempests and Whittinghams.

The surrounding agricultural land was classified as wasteland until the Lanchester Common Enclosure Plan of 1776. Enclosed farms such as New Acres were created and cereal crops were set. The land was then let to tennant farmers.

The Holmside Estates were sold in 1829 to William Bell & Partners. These included J. Morrison, William Hedley and G. Hunter, and they formed the South Moor Coal Co Ltd. This group mostly mined the northern section of this estate. In 1839 they leased the southern section to W. Hedley for £50 per annum. This area of land included South Moor, Craghead and Burnhope. Hedley began at once to sink the William Pit at Craghead and the West Craghead Colliery, later known as the William Pit, at South Moor.

There was massive migration into the area by miners and their families from all over Great Britain and Ireland. These people, all of different backgrounds and cultures, formed that special breed of man the 'Durham Miner'. They even developed their own language, known as 'pitmatic', which is slightly less harsh than 'Geordie'. They also created some words common only to North Durham.

William Hedley invented the first economical steam-powered locomotive in the country, long before Stephenson. By 1913 he had perfected two engines, the 'Puffing Billy' and the 'Wylam Dilly'. The latter worked at Craghead Colliery. Hedley brought his inventive mind to Craghead and South Moor Coalfields. The early-built houses for the miners and their families were little more than brick shelters to keep out the prevailing cold wind and the inclement weather. The houses had two rooms, the upper only accessible by ladder. The rooms had no ceilings and the lower room was paved with red flagstones. Between the rows of houses were ash pits and closets (toilets). The bricks were from Craghead Brick Works. Larger than expected coal deposits persuaded the coal owners to build two-bedroom houses of better quality to retain their workforce. Boulder clay was later found near the Charlie Pit and a new brickworks replaced the one at Craghead. These new, larger houses had an ashpit and primitive toilet at the end, known locally as 'the Netty'. They were replaced with water closets at the turn of the century.

Education was provided in 1847 at Holmside National School, situated between Wilkinsons Bank and Craghead on Wagtail Lane. A further school was added on the same site in 1877 by the Coal Co. In 1900, with a rapidly increasing population, a new school opened at Old South Moor, and the National School closed.

Tradesmen and shopkeepers came into the area. The roads were improved. Churches began to open, the Wesleyans at Old South Moor, the Central Primitive Methodists next to the colliery offices, and the New Connexion at Greenland. The Church of England erected St. Georges at South Moor and St. Thomas' at Craghead. The catholics held services at Hustledown Roman-Catholic School until they built St. Mary's. There was also the Salvation Army and the Spiritualists.

The earliest public house in the district was 'The John Castle Inn' at Craghead, followed in the mid-1800s by 'The Smith's Arms', 'The Oak Inn' and 'The Stag Inn'. Working Men's Clubs began circa 1900.

This mining community both worked and played hard, producing some fine sportsmen in football, cricket, handball etc. There were also bare knuckle fighting, cock fighting, pigeon racing, whippets, cycling, athletics, etc. At work they would talk of sport and the pub, and at weekends they would talk about the pit!

The womenfolk had a very hard life at home, with no leisure. There were no electricity, central heating or washing machines. No TVs or radios. They had little money to feed large families, they washed the clothes by hand and had tin baths in front of the fire. There was no Health Service or Social Security. There was real, general hardship and always the fear of sickness or lay-offs. They were loyal to each other's needs, a community spirit created through necessity, which has lasted over the years. Many would have expected the population to leave after the closure of the mines, but the area refused to die. The strength of the district was indeed 'The People'.

We would like to thank those who have contributed to this book. Our group pays special tribute to former local historian Mr. Fred Wade (deceased), who, by his work, has been our main inspiration in our quest to record local history.

New members are always welcome.

Jack Hair

1   New Acres Farm.

This is situated at the top of Wilkinsons Bank. The name New Acres was given at the time of the Lanchester Common Enclosure Plan in 1776. The area was formerly under the control of Lanchester Parish and became part of Holmside Parish in 1865. Directories of the 1850s state Wilkinsons farmed Morrow Field and the name Wilkinsons Bank has carried on.

2 Morrow Edge Cottages.

These cottages were built on New Acres when Joseph Oldfield was granted a stone quarry at Morrow Edge by the Church Commissioners in 1781. He erected two cottages and a blacksmiths. One of the cottages burned down in 1889 killing Betty Waugh. The other building was demolished in 1957.

3   Holmside National School.

This was the first school in the area situated on Wagtail Lane. It was erected in 1847 and further extended in 1877 by the Coal Co. For many years it was also used as a church. The first head teacher was Mr. J. Dixon followed by Mr. J. Lowe. The girls from this school transferred in 1893 to the former Infants' School at South Moor. The National School closed in December 1900, when a new mixed school was erected at Old South Moor.

4 The William Pit.

In 1829 South Moor Coal Co. was owned by J. Morrison, W. Bell, W. Hedley and G. Hunter. They purchased the Holmside Estate and leased the southern section to William Hedley for £50 per annum. He began sinking the William Pit at South Moor in 1839. It was first named the West Craghead Colliery, later to be named New South Moor Colliery and eventually the William or Billy Pit.

5   The William Pit.

A waggonway was made from the pit up to Oxhill Standing Engine near Oxhill Farm. The first coals went away on 25 July 1848. The wagons crossed the road at Oxhill and joined the Shield Row Waggonway at Pea Farm. The pit closed in 1864 but was remoduled and reopened in 1898. The coals were then sent by endless tubway across to the Hedley Pit and by wagonway to the Louisa. This system again changed in 1947, when the coals went directly underground to the Louisa.

6 Ellwood's Sweet Shop.

This shop owned by Cumberland born Belle Ellwood was at Old South Moor. The shop was in the living room and sweets were displayed on a table in the window. Her husband was former wrestler Marshall (Mash) Ellwood. In the picture are their children: Sarah Annie, Lucy, Jane and William Fletcher. Local children such as Fred Wade would get ½ penny once a fortnight pocket money and their first call would be to the Bullet Shop.

7 The Wesleyan Methodist Church.

A small chapel was erected in 1858 next to the Stag Inn. A larger church was soon needed and the foundation stone for this was laid on 4 December 1895 and the new church opened in 1896. The old church was used for a while by the Salvation Army and later pulled down. The church was later known as the Trinity Methodists, but later closed with the amalgamation of Methodist Churches. It was a builders' depot for some years and was bought in the early 1990s by the Jehovas Witnesses, who restored the building into the Kingdom Hall.

8 St. George's Church.

In the 1860s, services were held in the Colliery Offices. By 1889 they were held in South Moor Infants' School. At a meeting in the Girls' School in 1896, they were informed that the Church Commissioners had donated £800 with a further £400, plus 3 acres of land from South Moor Coal Co, towards a church and churchyard. The proposed church was modelled on the church at Nevilles Cross. The first tenders for building were too expensive, so the contract was split between A. Routledge (building) £1,092, and H. Mole (joinery etc) £519. The foundation stone was laid on 21 April 1897 and the dedication service took place on 30 March 1898.

9 St. George's Church.

The first Baptisms held at St.Georg's on 3 April 1898 were those of Ernest Pearson, John Rainbow Oldfield, M.E. Taylor, Mary and Jane Forster and Rachel and Elizabeth Clifford. The first marriage on 4 April 1898 was between William Ward and Annie Trotter. The first burial was that of William Greathead, aged 6. Vicars and Curates were: 1896-1900 C.J. Gray; 1900 J. Collins and G. Helliwell; 1902-1948 F.S. Myers; 1949-1953 H.V. Chisholm; 1953-1958 T. Barber; 1959 S. Royal (died in office); 1961-1968 P. Dearne; 1969-1972 J.W. Shewan; 1972-1977 Hoskins; 1978-1985 J.P. Troop; 1986-1995 Father Percy.

10 South Moor Primitive Methodist Church.

The Primitive Methodists held services in their own homes prior to 1894. Fund raising events were held in Oxley the butchers' hay loft. A small church was built and opened next to the Colliery Offices on 11 February 1894. It cost £430. A larger amphitheatre-type church was designed by J. Davison of Newcastle and built by J. Craven of Pelton. The new church opened in 1900 and the old small chapel became the schoolroom. Nelsons installed an organ costing £220 in 1909, and electric lights were installed in 1920, costing £91. The church was re-named the Central Methodists in 1932 and finally closed in 1962.

11   The Home Guard.

This photograph of Officers and NCOs was taken adjacent to the Colliery Offices at South Moor. Included from left to right are, back row: Ralph Daglish, unknown, W. Eagle, Cecil Hind, unknown and Rutherford the dentist. Front row: Ernie Eagle, Dick Simms, Arthur Thompson, Tommy Baker and Percy Kelly.

12 The Diamond Bus.

There were many different bus operators from Stanley to Quaking Houses. These included Hather Bell, French's Yellow Belly, Hammells, Mowbrays and Northern. This photo shows Mrs. Hammell at Fourth Street, Quaking Houses, in front of their Bedford bus. It was well renowned for the number of passengers these buses could hold. They never failed to pick up passengers and competed fiercely with the much larger Northern. 'Move up the bus' was the call!

13   The Charlie Pit.

This colliery was situated west of South Moor on land of Quaking Houses Farm. It was sunk in 1845 by William Bell and Partners and the photo shows the sinkers. It was first named New Shield Row Colliery, then Quaking Houses Pit. It later became known as the Charlie Pit. The first coals were sent away in 1846 when the Pea Pit closed. A large Waddle fan was installed in 1893. This was replaced with a high speed Sirocco fan in 1907.

14 The Charlie Pit.

The colliery had its own brickworks. There was an abundance of clay in the surrounding area. The largest quarry was to the rear of the Upper Standards School. The quarry closed in 1948 and levelling began. The last chimney, which was a local landmark, was demolished in 1975 when children of Greenland School were allowed by head teacher O Barrass, to witness the demolition.

15 Park Road Methodist Church.

This church, formerly New Connexion, was once named the Zion Church. Prior to the church, they held services in Oxleys Long Room. They obtained a site in the corner of a field known as Greenlands. They erected a corrugated iron church there, which opened on 29 July 1898. In 1907, there was a union between the United Methodists Free Church, the Methodist New Connexion and the Bible Christians. An amalgamation took place in the Stanley District in 1917, forming part of the United Methodist Church.

16 Park Road Methodist Church.

By 1917, the debt for the original church was cleared and they were fund raising for a new church which opened in 1933. This church cost £1,500, which excluded the price of the bricks which were provided free by South Moor Coal Co. The stone laying ceremony was on 3 December 1932 and the church opened on 15 July 1933. The rostrum and pews were acquired from Blackhill Methodist Church. The surrounding wall was erected by James Todd of Oxhill in 1933. The doors of the new church were opened by R.W. Cooper.

17 The Stag Inn.

This inn is listed in Hagars Directory of 1851 and was first built as an ale house. In 1851, this area was under Greencroft. The Oak, then owned by brewer Oxley, was called The Board. The two inns adjacent were listed as John Nattrass of the South Moor Red Lion, and Peter Welch of the South Moor New Inn. One of these was eventually renamed the Stag Inn. The family most renowned with the Stag Inn was the Lumley family and it became known locally as 'Revvy Lumleys'.

18　South Moor football team 1911-1912.

The Old Moor team were Cup and League winners in this season. In the back row are: head teacher J. Lowe, with teachers Herdman, Gray, Donaghy and Thompson. The players were: Greener, R. Middlemass, D. Lee, T. Swinburne, J. Purdy, J. Middlemass, C. Gowland, J. Khulman, T. Shelley, T. Beckworth, Savage, Cummings and H. Frost. The school also won the cricket trophy that year. Mr. Lowe retired shortly after this.

19   Greenland School football team 1929.

This school was well known for its sporting achievements, especially football. Over the years they won many competitions and trophies. Pictured here in 1929 were: J. Robinson, H. Woolcock, L. Liddle, A. Phillips, W. Siddle, J. Bell, F. Wright, J. Curtiss, G. Maddison, unknown, Mountain and E. Briggs.

20 The Hedley Pit.

This pit was sunk in 1885 on land to the left side going up the bank towards the Old Moor. On 29 September 1930, a coal hewer named Fred Beaumont was entombed by a fall of stone. Nineteen fellow workmen did valiant work before he was rescued. In February 1932, these brave men received the Edward Medal from His Majesty King George V.

21 **The Hedley Pit boilers.**

This photo shows staff at the boilers around 1926. There was also an event in the 1920s at this pit when over 150 men were trapped underground for two days due to a breakdown in the shaft. Due to the state of disrepair to the escape way to the small shaft at Kitley Nook near Ashley Park, only a few men per hour could be brought to the surface. There were no injuries at this incident.

22 The Fell Pit, Burnhope.

The Burnhope Pits were sunk by Hedley in 1844. He later sold them to Soulsby & Fletcher. They disposed of them to U.A. Ritson in 1881. They then came under the ownership of Holmshaw and Partners, who sold them on to Bearpark Coal Co. The colliery was nationalised in 1947 and closed in 1949. In earlier days a wagonway to Craghead from Burnhope was completed in 1844. The Morrow Edge standing engine was built in 1845.

23   Parry's lorries.

These lorries are shown standing at the Charlie Pit ready for hire. They worked mostly from the nearby coal depot. These lorries transported coal throughout the area and to the miners homes. In the background are Oxhill Methodist Church and Oxhill Farm.

24 South Moor Excelsior Working Men's Club.

This club was formed in 1908 when 200 members paid 2/6d each to join. The premises were opposite the South Moor Hotel in what was formerly Tommy Wright's greengrocery shop. The first club steward was William Brown and the first secretary was W.E. Atkinson. In 1924 the club moved to a wooden structure on the present site and traded there until 1938 the brick structure was built. The club celebrated the 50th anniversary in 1958.

25 Dale's Shop.

This view up South Moor Lane shows Dale's Shop. The Dale brothers were general dealers, well known for their bacon, cheeses, blended teas and freshly-ground coffee, which you could smell when entering their shop. They also traded in Stanley. They did home deliveries and many a young lad thrilled to the joy of riding Dale's bike!

26   South Moor Silver Prize Band.

The band was formed in 1892 and was poorly equipped for the first twelve years. In 1903 they purchased a Class A Besson Set. From 1904, under the professional instruction of W. Heap, they soon began to win competitions such as the Dunston Cup. In 1907, under the instruction of Gus Haigh, they won the Grand Shield at Crystal Palace, qualifying for the Championship Class. The band is shown in the 1930s.

27 The Garden House Club.

This club got its name from its early formation in the allotment gardens between South Moor and Stanley in the early 1900s. They moved from this wooden hut into newly-built 39 Spen Street on 3 January 1913. They had to pay over £60 for a license. They transferred to Tyne Road about 1933 and the former Spen Street club was converted into flats and sold for £255 to Mr. and Mrs. Scanlan. The photograph shows the committee and others outside the Tyne Road Club.

28 Wilson the blacksmith.

Although the area was predominantly a mining area, there were still many surrounding farms. These were worked mostly by horses, making the need for a village blacksmith. Mosey Wilson was the first of three generations of blacksmiths in South Moor from early 1905. He moved to the present smithy in 1912. He is shown here with his striker. The small child in the photo is Billy Renwick. The man at extreme right is Wilf Lees. Most of their work was shoeing horses and making and repairing farm implements.

29 Wilson the blacksmith.

Ernie Wilson senior was the son of Mosey Wilson. He took over as blacksmith from his father in 1936, although he had worked with him before this. Even with less shoeing there was still plenty of farm work. Ernie was commissioned to make the wrought iron gates for Annfield Plain Park. The Council was well pleased with his work. His son, Ernie, became the third generation blacksmith in South Moor when he took over in 1975. He was formerly a fitter/turner at Vickers before joining his father. He still trades in South Moor.

30 South Moor Social Club.

It is known locally as 'Mickey's' due to its original owner, Mr. Michael Martin. He purchased the site from the Towneley Estates. He held a license for an off-license and shop but was turned down for a full license for the new building. He formed a private club in the early 1900s, but this venture failed. A few of those members held a meeting on 15 October 1904 to form a Working Men's Club. They leased the land and building on a five year lease at £95 per annum and later purchased the building for £2,000. This club underwent major alterations in 1955 and moved to new premises in Severn Crescent in 1981.

31 South Moor Women's Institute.

They formed in 1932 in St. George's Church Hall. The first President was Mrs. W. Scott. They acquired a large wooden structure from the company who built Burnhope Reservoir. This building was officially opened by Mr. Basil Sadler in April 1937. It was situated west of Elm Street. Mr. Dawson, a former native of South Moor, gave £20 for every £100 raised and South Moor Coal Co. loaned the balance interest free. This hall was named the Coronation Hall.

32 South Moor Operatic Society.

They formed in 1933 under the guidance of Mrs. Myers, the wife of Canon Myers of St. George's Church. She and others gathered to form the Society. Sadly, Mrs. Myers died before they performed the first production, HMS Pinafore. In those early days they made their own costumes. They formed a drama section which was equally popular. Two of the original members, Miss A. Renwick and Mr. W. Pentney, received NADA medals for their service to the society, as have many others since then. The photo shows them in one of their early productions.

33 Stella Bridge.

This bridge was erected in 1905 to provide a safe crossing to South Stanley following the death on the railway of a young girl named Dodds. The building to the right was originally West Stanley Co-operative Bakery, which was the first building in Stanley to have electric lights. It later became the Boot & Shoe Factory. To the left of the photo was the Co-Op building, funeral and paint store. This bridge was demolished in 1964 and levelled the following year.

34 MacPhails the barbers.

This is another family who have served South Moor and Stanley for several generations. Mr. Hughie MacPhail came to the area in the early 1890s from Burbank in Hamilton. He was an outstanding personality. His first shop was on the Arcadia side of the street. This picture shows his shop on the other side. Note the barbers pole and the name 'Macs'. His prices before the war were: shaving 2d, haircut 3d, boys 2d, with no hair cutting on Saturdays. He died aged 68 in 1948 while visiting his sister in Edinburgh.

35 Hughie MacPhail junior.

He began working in his fathers shop aged 13. He is pictured here in his Park Road shop. Like his father, he was also well known and respected. The barber shop was more like a community centre, where men would drop in to join in the topic of the day. Hughie's son John and his wife Joan have salons in South Moor and East Stanley, so the tradition goes on. His nephews Colin and Keith also still trade in Stanley as hairdressers, having worked for many years with their father, Bob. Sister Tissie also had a salon in South Moor.

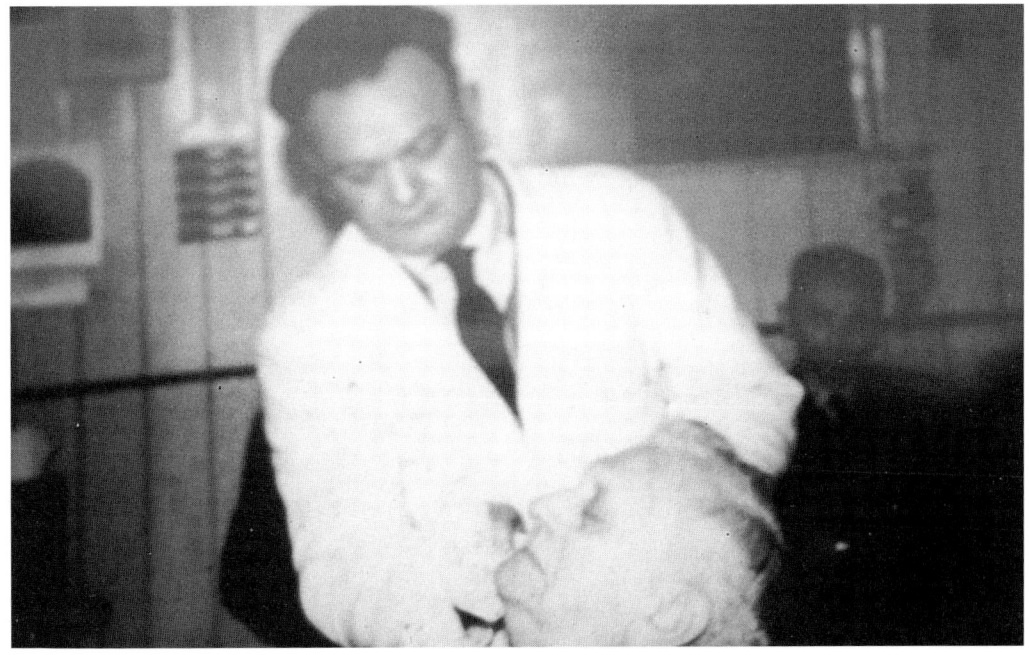

36 South Moor Arch.

It was first constructed as a stone arch for the Stanhope & Tyne Railway in 1833 and was replaced by a girder bridge as shown here in 1844. Prior to 1920 the road down from the Arch was known as Tommy's Lonnen and, later, South Moor Lane. It was renamed Park Road after the opening of the Memorial Park. Prior to this the streets either side of this road had different names, such as Widderington, Tempest, Dover, Poulton. Although the bridge was demolished in 1964 it is still known as the Arch, causing much confusion to strangers!

37 South Moor Hotel.

Mr. Oxley, a local brewer and innkeeper, owned the Oak Inn at Old South Moor. As more houses were being built at New South Moor, he decided to build a much larger, new hotel, as shown here. He transferred the license from the Oak Inn to the South Moor Hotel, which opened 10 December 1897. A new club room was opened in 1910. Before the Second World War there was a very active gymnasium and weight lifting club upstairs. Note, the hotel then had two doors at the front.

38 Burnhope Cricket Team.

Burnhope Village was renowned for sporting activities, including cricket. It was usual in coal mining villages for the colliery officials and the miners to unite in sport. This team of 1930 was one such and included: Bill Morallee, John Casson, J. Snaith (Colliery manager), J. Patterson, Jackie Dobson, Tom Patterson, W. Hovvells, Harry Hovvells, Norman Burnett, Harry Laverick, Jonty Fish, Billy Hoult and scorer Jackie Wood.

39 South Moor Cricket Club.

This club formed in 1884. They used to play their matches in a field at New Acres Farm until 1900, when they moved to their present site. The first team in 1902 won the Durham County Cup against Philadelphia at Chester-le-Street. The scores were: South Moor 103, Philadelphia 79. In that South Moor team were four players who represented their county: J. Fairley, A. Gowland, M. Cornbey and J. Cornbey.

40 South Moor Cricket Club 1929.

In this year they were champions of the North West Durham League for the nineth time in their history. That team was: F. Reed, Secretary, W. Roxby, J. Douglas, Umpire, J. Sample, T. Urwin, J. Daglish, J. Rutherford, W. Pomeroy, J. Dodds, A. Thompson, J. Fairley and W. Turner. The last two names are not known at the time of writing. South Moor still boasts a cricket team in the Tyneside Senior League and has been in existence for over a hundred years.

41 **South Moor Co-Operative Store.**

This was a branch of West Stanley Co-Op Society. This grand building was erected and opened on 18 August 1900 due mainly to the building of many new houses and a large increase in the population. On opening day there was a large parade of decorated carts from Stanley. In the afternoon the local children were treated to sports, games and a picnic in the Store Field. For those not visiting the shop there was always the store cart, which called weekly around the surrounding streets.

42 South Moor Co-Operative Greengrocery Department.

This early photo of the greengrocery department was propably taken not long after the branch opened. Below ground level were huge basement rooms used for the slaughter of cattle and livestock, and storage facilities for the various departments. After closure, the old building was taken over by Pinkhams glove factory and, later, the Mason Group. After standing empty for many years it is now to be demolished to make way for single persons accommodation. Its removal will make the building sadly missed by many locals, who remember their days shopping at the store.

43   Quaking Houses Co-Op Branch.

Due to the building of Third and Fourth Streets, the population of this area had greatly increased, so they decided to open a branch at Quaking Houses. This shop was situated in Third Street. The architect was Rownthwaite and the builder was Rutter. This branch opened 17 December 1921, saving the local people the long trip to either South Moor or Stanley. The first house shop in the long streets was supposedly in 27 Third Street in 1915.

44 Hedleys Wylam Dilly.

The engine is pictured here at Craghead in the late 1870s. William Hedley was born at Newburn in 1779. He was viewer at Walbottle and, later, also at Wylam Colliery. He discovered and demonstrated the efficiency of traction by smooth wheel on smooth wheel. He tried his first engine, built by Thomas Salters in 1813, but this engine was short of steam power. In May 1813 his second engine, the Puffing Billy, was fitted with a return boiler. He built the Wylam Dilly at the same time and these engines ran between Wylam and Tyne Staithes. The Hedleys brought the Wylam Dilly to Craghead Colliery in 1862, where it worked until 1879. It was then sent to the Chambers Museum in Edinburgh.

45   Craghead British Legion.

The Discharged Soldiers and Sailors Federation was formed after the First World War. The Craghead Branch held their meetings in the original iron church of St. Thomas on the site of the present vicarage. They moved to a wooden hut at Bloomfontein and in 1921 they became known as the British Legion. One of the original members, Michael Heavisides, was awarded the Victoria Cross for bravery. Other members, R. Blaney, W. Carr junior, E. Dodds and J.J. Lee, were awarded the Military Medal. The club was rebuilt in brick in 1954 and renamed Craghead Social Club.

46 Craghead Colliery Band.

This band was formed in 1910 with the help of the colliery owners. Two of the official functions of the band were to lead the funeral procession of any miner killed at Craghead Colliery, and to lead the Miners Lodge and banner at the Durham Miners Gala Day. They gave concerts in the open space of Front Street, between Wilsons the Cobbler's and Buckton's Shop. The band won their section at Belle View, Manchester, in 1913, and the North of England Championships in 1924. There were three members of the Carlyn Family in that band. After closure in 1968, the band was renamed Craghead Ever Ready.

47 Craghead Rifle & Sports Club.

Circa 1906, volunteers dug out the foundations for the club building next to the Hedley Memorial Hall. The Rifle Club members were equipped with 22 Lee Enfield rifles, later changing to competition BSA rifles. They had two teams in local leagues. In winter the matches were held indoors, but in summer they used the outdoor range near White House Farm. Six members of the team once scored 599 out of a possible 600 points. Joe, Jack and Richard Smith were very active in the club. The club had a gymnasium which was regarded as one of the best in the north for boxing and wrestling.

48 Craghead Co-Operative Society & the Punch Bowl.

Both are shown here circa 1920. The Co-Op had departments for grocery, hardware, boot and shoe, drapery, butchers, greengrocers and savings. There were a storeyard, stables and, upstairs, the famous Penny Gaff Cinema. The Punch Bowl was supposedly a small pub attached to a house on the same site as the present pub, which has been extensively modernised in recent years. The Co-Op was demolished in February 1992, but the old greengrocers is still standing, now D. Drills, and the stable block is a garage.

49 Front Street, Craghead.

This is a view of Front Street circa 1920. On the left of the photo is the John Castle Inn, a listed building, thought to have been a coach house circa 1686. On the right is a selection of shops and other buildings: Race, grocer and newsagent, Oswald, butcher, the hotel known locally as Sammy Leightons, Craghead Victoria Working Men's Club, and Maughans fish shop. The first block is now North View Nursing Home. The hotel is now Noel Wilson's Printing Works. The fish shop is now Armstrongs, general dealers.

50 **The Mitchison family.**

The Mitchisons have farmed the surrounding countryside for over 150 years. One of the farms worked by John Mitchison and his wife was Fawside Farm near Craghead. John is pictured here at Fawside, sewing grass seed with his fiddle bow seeder. In the background is St. Thomas' Church. John bought the fiddle seeder as a young man and was greatly amused that, when he retired, he sold the implement at a profit!

51 Hustledown Welfare Ambulance.

Prior to the opening of Holmside & South Moor Hospital, the local Miners Welfare Fund was used to provide motor-driven ambulances. Until then, injured miners were transported either to their homes or to Newcastle Infirmary in straw-lined horse-drawn carts. Many died on the long journey and the introduction of the motor ambulance greatly improved their chances of survival. The ambulance seen here, driven by Mr. Cresswell, was kept for a while at Hustledown Rescue Station, although others were based at the Pit Head.

52 South Moor Roman-Catholic Infant and Junior School.

This school, known later as St. Mary's, was erected by Father Dix in 1911, and opened 11 June that year with 81 pupils. The head teacher was Miss M. Walmsley. The caretaker's house was built shortly after. Church services were held within the school. In 1913, a Junior/Senior School was built adjacent, although both schools had separate head teachers. The head of the new school was Miss E. Conway, and this school opened 18 August 1913, with 156 pupils. Both schools amalgamated in 1947. The present head teacher is Mrs. Mary Allan.

53 Hustledown Miners' Rescue Team.

The Station was built by South Moor Coal Co. in 1912/13 and was well stocked with every type of underground rescue equipment. There was breathing apparatus, lifting gear, hoists, jacks and even canaries used in the likely event of gas. This photo shows the rescue team shortly after winning a competition.

54 South Moor Memorial Park.

The park was opened by Mr. R.W. Cooper on 10 July 1920 on land gifted by South Moor Coal Co. It was named Memorial Park in honour of the men of South Moor who gave their lives in the Great War 1914-1918. Their names are engraved in the stonework at each side of the ornate gates. The Colliery Band gave weekly concerts in the park grandstand, when huge crowds turned out to hear them.

55   Holmside & South Moor Welfare Fund Hospital.

The Miners' Act of 1920 was passed compelling coal owners to pay an annual fee of 1d per tonne to a Welfare Fund for the benefit of the miners. Local lodges proposed to use the money for a hospital. Thomas Lumsden was awarded the building contract and work began in 1925. The bricks were supplied from South Moor Coal Co. and work was completed in 1926, costing £24,092 5s 8d. The official opening by D.M.A. leader Mr. Robson was held on 29 June 1927. Miners' offtakes were used for the upkeep of the hospital.

56 The Smiths Arms.

This pub at the top of the Old Moor bank was listed in the 1851 Directories, but is probably much older than that. It closed for many years and was reopened by local sportsman Jack Mutton when the Hedley Pit began in the 1850s. Saturday was the main day when there was handball, quoits, short distance pigeon racing, pitch and toss, rabbit coursing, pigeon shooting and bare knuckle fighting. In a room behind the Smiths Arms, W. Maddison arranged cock fighting.

57 The Louisa Pit coal lorries.

The lorries are shown here under the coal hoppers at the Louisa. The coals from the Hedley Pit were hauled by endless ropeway up the east side of South Moor to the Louisa. The bulk of the coal would then go by rail down the Pontop & Shields Railway. Local deliveries went by horse-drawn cart until the introduction of these early lorries.

58 South Moor Post Office.

This was one of the early buildings in New South Moor in 1892. The block of buildings consisted of Trotters the butcher, J. Pringle the tailor, and John Smith, postmaster. Letters and parcels were collected by a one-horse-drawn cart and taken to Chester-le-Street via the Old Moor and Craghead. Mr. Smith was a member of the Stanley Board in 1892 and became a councillor for eighteen years on Stanley Council. He was a JP and a churchwarden for thirty years at St. George's Church. He died on 2 May 1931 aged 90 and was succeeded by his son-in-law, Robert Moore.

59 The Coronation Car.

This was a fine 33 seater charabanc built at Luton, costing £1,000. It was then the biggest bus built in Britain and was owned by Mr. Martin of South Moor. It was open sided and on the roof was painted 'Coronation Car'. It was involved in North West Durham's worst road accident on 26 August 1911 when nine people died and many were injured. They were with Consett Co-Op Choir on the way to Prudhoe Flower Festival. The brakes of the bus overheated and disintegrated going down Long Close Bank near Medomsley. Mr. Wilson, the driver, stayed at the wheel before finally losing control.

60 South Moor Loco Mishap.

The photo shows a crowd of local people gathering to see the South Moor Colliery locomotive which went over the top of the coal depot at South Moor. It crashed to the ground but, surprisingly, no-one was badly hurt. This accident happened on Derby Day 1920. The driver was Mr. James Brown. The engine was sent to Hawthorne Leslie on Tyneside for repair and it was later returned to South Moor.

61 South Moor Miners' Hall.

This was opened in 1898 by MP John Wilson. The first caretaker was Mat Robinson. The Hall had reading rooms, games and billiards rooms and also a library. The large hall was always in great demand for dances, concerts, etc. Variety shows were staged by Mr. Carlyn, who also showed the first animated picture show in the area. The building is now owned by Mr. D. Bragan.

MINERS HALL, SOUTH MOOR.

62 **The Pomeroys.**

These are one of the longest established families in Craghead. Mr. Pomeroy senior came from Cornwall to work in the local mines. He later went into business including haulage, farming, shopkeeping, deliveries, and horse-drawn buses. He also had a funeral service. This photo of 1929 shows, from left to right: Ed Pomeroy as a young lad, his uncle Charlie, who farmed Ousterly Farm, Jack Grix, and Ed's father Joseph Pomeroy, who farmed Low Ousterly Farm. The horses were Belgian Blacks, which the family used on the farm for haulage and for funerals.

63 Gowland's shop.

This was situated at what is now Hamfletts newsagent, and part of Watsons hardware store on Park Road. They were quality hat makers and suppliers of gents' clothes. It was considered a very good hat that had the Gowland label inside! The name Gowland can still be seen in the ornate step in the entrance to Hamfletts.

64   Tates shop and adjoining house.

The house was for many years occupied by Thomas and Agnes Buller. They brought up a large family in this old building which had no gas or any modern facilities. The house and shop were finally demolished in the 1940s and the Buller family was rehoused. Beyond the fields are Muriel Street and Wardle Street.

65   Tates confectionary shop.

This small shop was situated at the lowest part of South Moor Lane. It was almost opposite the Miners' Hall, in the area that is now the playing fields. There were steps down to the shop and the adjacent house, and the Burn ran alongside.

66 The Arcadia Cinema.

In this street scene we see the shops of L. Welsh, J.T. Stevens, Millers and the Arcadia Cinema. This cinema opened on 24 March 1914. There were two other cinemas in South Moor, the Tivoli, which opened on 18 June 1922, and the Picture Hall in Rose Avenue, which opened in 1912. The last picture shown at the Arcadia was 'Best of Enemies' on 1 September 1962. Cinema shows were then transferred to the Tivoli, which had been closed for one year. The Arcadia then became a bingo hall.

67   The Hedley Pit coal hewers.

This is a photo of the Hedley Pit coal hewers just before going down the mine. The coal hewer was a special breed of man. In early days he would be equipped with a coal shovel, a cracket and a piece of timber, holed to take the drilling machine. He had to provide his own pick and shaft and explosives. He would buy the black powder at the Co-Op and make his own cartridges at home, carrying them to the pit in a shot box. He also carried a candle box fitted with a lid. His bait would be a bottle of water and sugared bread. Some men had small naked-light oil lamps with a hood called a 'midge lamp', while others worked by candle light.

68 Shield Row drift mine.

This was situated between Quaking Houses and the Charlie Pit. The coals from the drift travelled to the south drift surface on to the north landing and along to Louisa Colliery. In this photo, the small building front left was the lamp cabin. The larger building in the centre was the manager's office and ambulance room, with the canteen nearby. At the top left of the picture is the end of the Drift Cottages. At one time these were occupied by the Platten family and the Shield family.

69 The Morrow Edge Evictions.

The police are shown here at Morrow Edge Cottages in 1933: an established colony of people living in broken down caravans and huts, which were little more than shanties. They had no water, light or sanitation. On 25 October, the council bailiff, J. MacKay, and a body of men assembled. The dwellings which could not be moved were burned out. The evicted people were lodged in public buildings until accommodation could be found.

70   St. Mary's Church, Hustledown.

The church, shown on the right, was built for the catholics of South Moor, Bloomfontein and Craghead in 1932. The architects were Messrs. Kitching of Middlesborough and the building contractor was H. Kindred of Sunniside. The foundation stone was laid by Dr. Joseph Thornton, Bishop of Hexham on 2 May 1932. The first priest in charge was Father Pickering. He was killed in a road accident in 1946 and was succeeded by Father Scriven.

71 Craghead Wesleyan Church.

A Mission Band held open air services in Craghead in 1890. Both the colliery and village were rapidly expanding. Colliery under manager Henry Bell suggested the need for a Wesleyan Church. He and Nicholas Musgrove and Henry Greener attended the Chester-le-Street Circuit meeting. By June 1891, regular house classes were being held in the home of Mrs. Crossman in Railway Street. In 1894, a small hall was acquired. Land for the present church was obtained from the Coal Co. and the church opened on 26 June 1897. The architect was Thompson of Newcastle and the builders were Isaac Oates of Chester-le-Street. The cost was £790, much of which was raised door to door by Mesdames Plummer and Greener.

72   The burn and Hustledown.

The burn was crossed by a wooden bridge. Quite often, after a storm of heavy rain, the burn would be heavily flooded. Sometimes it was impassable. Occasionally, the pupils from Hustledown School would be allowed home early so they could cross the burn before the floods became too bad. This burn is now filled in, and there is a more sturdy bridge.

73 PCs Stubbs & Vittee.

Circa 1900, they were policemen employed by South Moor Coal Co. and they were housed in colliery property. PC Vittee lived in Cement Rows at Annfield Plain. PC Stubbs was the first policeman to live in South Moor at 1 Poplar Street. As most of the area was owned by the coal owners, including farms, collieries, houses and offices, they had a large area to cover. Their job was not made easy due to the pubs being open from early morning until late at night.

74   South Moor Colliery Offices.

These were built opposite South Moor Co-Op to replace the old William Pit Offices in 1906. The manager's house called 'The Limes' was part of this building and supposedly the first house in South Moor to have a bathroom. Pay day was once a fortnight. The Friday pay day was like a social event. Local traders would often wait there to collect money owing to them over the previous two weeks.

75   Heslops confectionary shop.

This shop was situated half way up South Moor Bank on the right-hand side going up to the Arch. It sold sweets and other confectionary and, before the re-naming of the street to Park Road, this short street was named Dover Tce. The shop is now owned by Vaymans.

76 Millers of South Moor.

This firm were high quality drapers. They started trading in South Moor in 1904 in a shop that later became Pattisons newsagents. They moved to the larger premises shown on the right of the photo in 1926, and these premises were later enlarged. This was the largest shop in the Moor after the Co-op, and traded there until recently when they moved the business to Stanley.